UNLEASH
YOUR *epic* SELF

35 Practices for Busting the Effort Myth

Sherri W. Fisher

Medfield, MA

 Positive Edge Press
An imprint of Sherri W. Fisher LLC
Medfield MA 02052

Copyright © 2022 by Sherri W. Fisher

All rights reserved. No part of this book may be reproduced in any form or by any electronic or mechanical means—except in the case of brief cited quotations embodied in articles or reviews—without written permission from the author. For product and distribution inquiries, please visit www.learnandflourish.com.

VIA Youth Survey ©Copyright 2004-2022, VIA Institute on Character. All Rights Reserved. Used with permission.

The POS-EDGE® Model: Sherri W. Fisher LLC/ Learn & Flourish LLC. All rights reserved. Used with permission.

UYES®: Sherri W. Fisher LLC/ Learn & Flourish LLC. All rights reserved. Used with permission.

Book design by Carla Green, Clarity Designworks

ISBN 978-1-7321368-3-0 (paperback)
ISBN 978-1-7321368-4-7 (ebook)

Disclaimer:
The advice and strategies found within this workbook may not be suitable for every situation. This book is designed to provide general educational information about the subjects discussed and not intended as a substitute for the diagnosis, treatment, cure, or prevention of any social, physical, psychological, or emotional condition, or as a substitute for the professional advice of a physician, psychologist, psychiatrist, or other expert's direct assistance.

Use of this book does not establish any type of advisory, counseling, or professional relationship with the author or publisher. References to other sources are provided for informational purposes only and do not constitute an endorsement of those sources. This work is sold with the understanding that neither the author nor the publisher is held responsible for the results accrued from the advice in this book.

While all attempts have been made to verify information provided for this publication, the publisher assumes no responsibility for errors, omissions, or contrary interpretation of the subject matter herein.

For more information visit https://learnandflourish.com

This book is about you
In it you are the writer of your own life
Unleashing Your Epic Self
in every exercise, reflection, and scribble space

May you learn from your challenges
Bust the effort myth
Grow in skill, self-awareness, and self-regulation
Flourish in all aspects of your life

Contents

What's Inside? vii

1 Positivity 1
    Notice What Went Well 4
    Spot Positive Emotion 6
    Savor What Went Well 8
    Bank on Positivity 10
    Be Grateful 12
    Expand on Positivity 14

2 Optimism and Resilience 15
    Tell New Stories 18
    Spot Your Thinking Traps 20
    Grow Your Mindset 22
    Mind Your Mind Chatter 24
    Build Hope 26
    Expand on Optimism and Resilience 28

3 Strengths 29
    Detect Your Strengths 32
    Spot Strengths Heroes and Sidekicks 34
    Manage Strengths Buttons 36
    Hitch Your Strengths to a Star 38
    Accomplish Together with Strengths 40
    Expand on Strengths 42

4 Emotional Intelligence 43
    Practice Self-Compassion 46
    Tell Me More 48
    Be Emotionally Contagious 50
    Commit Acts of Kindness 52
    Give Up on Grudges 54
    Expand on Emotional Intelligence 56

5 Decision Making and Change 57
Be Your Own Boss 60
Train and Care for Your Elephant.............................62
Cue New Habits..64
If This, Then That 66
Manage Procrastination..68
Expand on Decision Making and Change.........................70

6 Goal Setting, Grit, and Growth Mindset
Follow the Three Rules for Adulting...........................74
Just Get Started Daily..76
Make a Growth Mindset Goal Plan 78
Reward Small Wins Regularly...................................80
Be Gritty and Accountable.....................................82
Expand on Goal Setting, Grit and Growth Mindset 84

7 Engagement and Exercise..........................85
Practice Mindfulness Meditation 88
Focus on Food, Exercise, and Sleep 90
Move: It's Good Medicine 92
Get Into Flow...94
Invest in Experiences 96
Expand on Engagement and Exercise 98

Appendix 99
My POS-EDGE Profile: Unleashing My Epic Self 101
Review and Reflect 102
Character Strengths 103

Inspiration and Gratitude 104
About the Author 105

What's Inside *Unleash Your Epic Self*?

Learning to manage well-being and work habits is as fundamental to life success as knowing how to read, write, and solve problems. To make improvements, of course, some effort is necessary. However, trying harder can become exhausting and discouraging. There is a better way.

Did you know that it's not how hard you try that leads to success? It's **how** you try harder that matters most.

Based on decades of well-being and productivity research, this newly updated edition of *Unleash Your Epic Self* helps adolescents and young adults establish resilience and self-direction skills while also nurturing strengths, relationships, and habits to support school, work, and life goals.

Inside you'll find seven well-being and productivity sections. Each one guides you through five easy-to-accomplish weekly practices—35 in all. Use the practices alone or with a group. Each section also has space to reflect on and extend your learning.

Start boosting your focus and busting the effort myth today.

» Mindfully notice what is going well, even when some things are not

» Respond to challenges with more resilient thinking, and less sadness and worry

» Spot, manage, and develop your strengths for success

» Strengthen your self-advocacy and relationship skills

» Build self-regulation and perseverance capacity

» Set goals and handle the challenges of procrastination

» Move toward the future you deserve with more calm, flow, and self-direction

Seven skill sections sharpen your Pos-Edge®:

Positivity
- » Notice what's good
- » Collect more positive than negative

Optimism and resilience
- » Expect what's good
- » Reframe what isn't

Strengths
- » Get more of what's good about you
- » Develop new strengths

Emotional intelligence
- » Develop solid relationships
- » Be grateful, forgiving, and kind

Decision making and change
- » Desire what's good
- » Manage obstacles to success

Goal setting, grit, and growth mindset
- » Plan for and stick with what's good
- » Unleash the power of YET

Engagement and exercise
- » Apply strengths and mindfulness
- » Invest in shared experiences

How *Unleash Your Epic Self* Helps Bust the Effort Myth

Do you or someone you care about spend more effort resisting work than just getting it done? It is so tempting to think that just trying harder can fix things.

I label this answer ***the effort myth***. It is a story that people tell about someone (maybe you!) who seems smart enough to be successful, but who is struggling to achieve.

The real way to improve is not just to put in more effort. It is knowing how to try differently that can help change things for the better!

In *Unleash Your Epic Self*, you can learn how to spend your efforts more effectively, and in ways that build your POS-EDGE® for well-being.

Each of the 35 *Unleash Your Epic Self* practices includes four steps:

Learn
- » Understand
- » Gain knowledge or skill

Grow
- » Connect and expand new learning
- » Make choices and personalize

Flourish
- » Practice abilities
- » Experience and apply them in new ways

Reflect
- » Look inward
- » Consider new action

> *It's not how hard you try that leads to success. It's **HOW** you try harder that matters most.*

SHERRI FISHER

SECTION ONE:
POSITIVITY

KEYS TO POSITIVITY
» Notice what's good
» Collect more positive than negative

Did you know that the ten most common positive emotions are joy, gratitude, serenity, interest, hope, pride, amusement, inspiration, awe, and love? Each time you experience one of these it adds to your well-being balance, just like in a savings account.

Positivity is your foundation for success. Happier people notice and appreciate what's going well. They also savor positive memories of the past and expect positive experiences in the future. It is easier for happier people to want to try new learning and study skills that can lead to things like sport, academic, and professional success.

People who are higher in positivity are also more grateful and forgiving in relationships. Other people report liking them better. Happier people tend to be more focused and organized, and they earn more money across their lifespan. They even tend to have longer and healthier lives. In short, happiness leads to success.

Positivity Practices

WEEK ONE

Notice What Went Well

WEEK TWO

Spot Positive Emotion

WEEK THREE

Savor What Went Well

WEEK FOUR

Bank on Positivity

WEEK FIVE

Be Grateful

WEEK ONE
Notice What Went Well

Learn
Happiness is made up of the many tiny moments of positive emotion that you feel every day. Sometimes it can feel as if you need to wait for random things to happen to be happier. Scientists have found out that when you train your brain to actively look for good things, you can become happier than by waiting for random events.

If you are happy with your life overall, you may already be noticing the good. Spending time paying attention to your positive life situation can make you even happier. If you want to be even more satisfied with your life, there are things that help.

Grow
Your brain is made up of very old parts that are wired for survival and newer parts that help you problem solve and use words effectively. Survival emotions include ones for fear and anxiety, guilt and shame, as well as ones for anger and disgust. These are useful, if not pleasant, emotions.

Negative emotions are "stronger" than positive ones, and they seem to stay with us longer, too. They are reinforced throughout every day in our thoughts and in our conversation. Fortunately, you can collect your positive thoughts to counterbalance this. Reinforce the good by choosing to actively focus on positive emotions and interactions. That's one way to build your well-being.

Flourish
NOTICE WHAT WENT WELL

Do you notice small pleasures each day? For most people about three positives are a good amount to counterbalance every one negative. Some people need more than three. You can experiment to find out your own positivity ratio.

Here's how to collect the positives and negatives so that you are more likely to have a positive ratio of thoughts and feelings. In the daily pages of your *Unleash Your Epic Self* workbook, you will have a chance to focus each day on "What Went Well". Train yourself to notice good things and record them. It is a powerful way to keep your ratio at 3:1 or more, and to find your own sweet spot.

Start by asking yourself this question:
What went well today?

Follow up with:
What was good about these things?

Then ask yourself:
How can I get more things like this?

Reflect

Small intentional choices you make build your well-being over time. That's why in addition to learning skills of well-being each week, your workbook gives you space to spot and record what helps you to unleash your epic self.

You might want to add the date or scribble notes about what's going well. Your "What Went Well" entries at the end of each practice can be something random ("I saw a double rainbow."; "I won free tickets.") or be about something you worked for ("I beat my best time ever." or "My project was a success." "They said yes!"). Choose the best things that happened during the week. Think about what you can do, and explore ways to take even little steps.

This week's practice was "Notice What Went Well".
ASK YOURSELF DAILY: What went well today?
　　　　　　　　　　　To get more of this I will . . .

WEEK TWO

Spot Positive Emotion

Learn

Despite research that shows how important it is to learn and use well-being builder activities, many people count on exciting positive events to get them through the day. They might hope for something big: that they will win a life-changing lottery prize, meet their perfect romantic partner, or have perfect weather for a big event. The truth is that only a small fraction of our happiness is the result of our life circumstances.

Grow

Close to half of your well-being can be affected by intentional activities—the ones *you* choose. Wish you had more control over your own life, to set goals, make choices, increase self-regulation? You have the greatest potential for unleashing your epic self when you learn skills to impact your own life every day. Some examples of intentional activities might include:

- Focusing on what is going well (even when some things aren't)
- Choosing flexible approaches when dealing with challenges
- Spotting and using your strengths
- Connecting with friends and loved ones
- Choosing activities that give you meaning and purpose
- Challenging yourself with goals and taking action toward them
- Engaging in regular exercise, healthy diet, and quality sleep

Can you make yourself happier by the things you do? Science says yes. Some people may be naturally happier than others, since heredity does give people a happiness set point. But only about half of happiness comes from our genes. Well-being improves when you can take charge in at least some ways.

Flourish

CUSTOMIZE POSITIVITY

You can customize many of your life choices, like the way you choose what you want on your part of a pizza.

1. Imagine a pizza with 10 slices. Five of them have toppings the pizza maker put on them. This is like heredity. One slice got toppings on it when the box corner was bumped on the way home. Sigh. It was beyond your control. This is like life circumstances that you cannot change. But four of the slices are still waiting for your toppings. This is where personal choices can increase positivity.

2. How can you make those four slices just right for you? What toppings will you choose for your Positivity Pizza? Think of things that will make you feel happier, and add them over and over again.

Reflect

Remember that small choices you make build your flourishing power over time. Unleashing your epic self depends on this! What went on your Positivity Pizza? What was good about that?

This week's practice was "Spot Positive Emotion".

ASK YOURSELF DAILY: What went well today?

                              To get more of this I will . . .

WEEK THREE

Savor What Went Well

Learn

Imagine that you could benefit from happy events more than the one time they happen. Savoring is like that. It is a way of enhancing what was, is, or will be going well, by choosing to actively enjoy and appreciate the experience.

Savoring is the deep enjoyment you experience when recalling and appreciating positive events from the past, being deeply attentive to what is wonderful in the present, or anticipating how a happy future event will make you feel. By choosing what to focus on and how you like to experience it, you can intensify your positive emotions. Awesome!

Grow

One way to savor the past is to recall a time when you were at your best. You could be at any age or stage in your life so far. Imagine in detail the events you recalled when you were at your best. Make the moment last, and deepen your feelings about this moment. Imagine your body moving and the sensations you felt. Remember how good it felt to be told what a fine job you had done. Recall the pleasurable sensations you felt during this happy moment.

Flourish

SAVORING YOURSELF AT YOUR BEST

Be grateful for the opportunity to be at your best, all over again. Here's how:

1. First, find a place that is relaxing for you. It could be inside or outside. You may want to do this while sitting still. Other people like to do this thought exercise while moving. Try seated, walking, jogging, or even showering.

2. Close your eyes. Start with a cleansing breath, inhaling slowly and deeply through your nose. Exhale. Repeat.

3. Now recall a time when you were at your best. Let good memories wash over you. Remember feeling most alive, most involved, or most excited. What made it an exciting experience? Who was involved? What made this experience come to mind?

Reflect

Imagine that you could relive any three epic moments in your life. What would they be, and why would you want to relive them?

This week's practice was "Savor What Went Well".

ASK YOURSELF DAILY: What went well today?

To get more of this I will . . .

WEEK FOUR
....

Bank on Positivity

Learn
Research shows us that regularly noticing the good things in our lives feels good: It builds positive emotion. Remember practicing savoring? It's one of the ways you can recycle your positive emotion. So while it is true that happy moments wear off quickly, and you may need three or more of them to counteract negative moments, your positivity is more than just a bunch of good feelings. Regular contributions to your positivity "bank" add up, and they protect you against the effects of negative emotions.

Grow
What makes happiness so powerful? Positive emotions work by doing what scientists call "broaden and build". They broaden or expand your willingness to consider new options. In this way interest or curiosity may help you to be willing to try something new. As a result, you may be challenged, and you will also learn and grow from the experience. Positive emotions also build up well-being over time, so when times are not so good, you have a cushion of good feeling to remind you that things were good before and can be again.

Flourish

MAKE DEPOSITS TO YOUR POSITIVITY BANK

Your positivity works like a savings account. Put in more than you take out and both your everyday and long-term happiness increase. What positive emotions are adding up in your "broaden and build" account? Thinking about today, rate the boost these activities give you.

- Connect with a friend
- Wear a favorite "something"
- Listen to your favorite song
- Accomplish a goal
- Reconsider a problem from a different point of view
- Stick with a plan
- Resist temptation
- Get invited somewhere
- Enjoy the weather
- What else?

Reflect

Looking at your week's activities, which ones gave you the biggest positivity boost? What was best for you about those experiences?

This week's practice was "Bank on Positivity".

ASK YOURSELF DAILY: What went well today?

To get more of this I will . . .

WEEK FIVE

Be Grateful

Learn
One of the most important positive emotions that you need for flourishing is gratitude. You have been quietly practicing it so far by noticing what has been going well; recalling the people, places, things, and events that have brought you happiness; and savoring them.

Most people like to be recognized for doing good things for others, so gratitude makes both the giver and the receiver happy, and it builds flourishing relationships. In many ways, gratitude is the ultimate positive emotion. For most people, it expands both their sense of well-being and belonging. It's good to feel genuinely grateful.

Grow
Close your eyes and think of things that make you laugh, smile, fist-pump, or say, "WOW." These could be places you've been, experiences you've had, people in your life, or precious moments in time. The thankful feeling this gives you is gratitude. It's the positive foundation of your relationships and well-being. Feeling grateful for what you do have and for what you can do, instead of comparing yourself to others, makes you nicer, more trusting, and more social. And here's a bonus: If you think grateful thoughts before bed, it can even help you sleep better. You'll feel even better tomorrow.

Flourish

FEEL AND SHARE GRATITUDE

Things that are rare often appreciate (increase) in value over time. Here are two ways to appreciate good experiences so that they appreciate and deepen.

Choose which one you will do:
1. Chances are that someone has been kind to you and that you appreciate it deeply. You might not have told the person, though. Write a letter of gratitude to someone and explain in detail why you are grateful to them. If you can, deliver it in person to share your gratitude. You could even read it to them. Journal about this in your reflection.

2. Keep up with your daily workbook pages. Notice what went well in your day. Write about it. Explain about what happened, what was good about it, and what you contributed to making the good thing happen. What would you do to get something else like this all over again?

Reflect

Did you write a gratitude letter this week? If not, pick someone you are grateful to and write it now. If so, what was it like for you? Did you deliver the letter and read it aloud to them before giving the letter to the other person?

This week's practice was "Be Grateful".

ASK YOURSELF DAILY: What went well today?

To get more of this I will . . .

EXTEND YOUR POSITIVITY
- » Notice what's good
- » Collect more positive than negative

POSITIVE EMOTIONS CHECKLIST

Use this checklist over and over to see what positive emotions you'd like even more of.

I'd like to feel more: *I can experience more of this positive emotion by:*

- » Amazement   _____
- » Anticipation   _____
- » Awe   _____
- » Bliss   _____
- » Cheerfulness   _____
- » Confidence   _____
- » Contentment   _____
- » Enjoyment   _____
- » Enthusiasm   _____
- » Excitement   _____
- » Exhilaration   _____
- » Gratitude   _____
- » Happiness   _____
- » Hope   _____
- » Interest   _____
- » Liveliness   _____
- » Love   _____
- » Peacefulness   _____
- » Pleasure   _____
- » Pride   _____
- » Relief   _____
- » Security   _____
- » Surprise   _____
- » _____   _____
- » _____   _____

SECTION TWO:
OPTIMISM AND RESILIENCE

KEYS TO OPTIMISM AND RESILIENCE
» Expect what's good
» Reframe what isn't

Optimism gives you thought power: a mindset of stronger coping skills for flourishing in the important areas of your life. When you are optimistic, you tend to think of failures as learning experiences. This helps you to actively search for and believe in potential solutions to even epically challenging situations. You can become more resilient and bounce back more quickly from discouragement.

What's an important ability that resilient people have learned? It's how to consider more than the first automatic negative thought that pops into their heads when something goes wrong! Too much information bombards you in challenging situations. You can benefit from mental shortcuts, but some of these lead to thinking traps.

Optimism and resilience let you practice flexible thinking and come up with alternative thoughts. Even if you are not naturally optimistic, you can learn the flexibility of resilient thinking. When you reframe the reasons things may not have worked out quite right, you can take better charge of managing pesky stresses and anxiety about the future.

Optimism and Resilience Practices

WEEK ONE

Tell New Stories

WEEK TWO

Spot Your Thinking Traps

WEEK THREE

Grow Your Mindset

WEEK FOUR

Mind Your Mind Chatter

WEEK FIVE

Build Hope

WEEK ONE
Tell New Stories

Learn
Most people think that optimism is about expecting good things to happen in the future. While that is partly true, what's more important is that optimistic people also imagine that they can positively influence the future. Before you get to imagining your future though, become more aware of the stories you tell yourself now. Those stories contain your explanations about why you think events, both good and bad, happen to you. Who or what caused them? How long will they be a problem? What things in your life are affected by the problem? What if you want to change things?

Grow
Your thoughts and explanations can strengthen the emotions you feel, both positive and negative ones. Say you are angry after an argument when you did not get your way. You may think about all of the reasons why you are right and the other person is wrong, and keep replaying that story, and those thoughts, in your head. You might tell the story to someone else so that they confirm for you that the explanation is right, and your situation is unjust. Together optimism and resilience are about managing those thoughts. They are a learned set of skills for dealing with times when you face negative thoughts, the kind that drag you down and keep you from positive action. These skills help you deal with:

- momentary negative emotions
- accumulated daily difficulties
- bigger setbacks

Flourish

THINKING ABOUT SETBACKS

Write about something that did not go well for you recently.

Take yourself back to the moment, and explain the thoughts and emotions you were having then, in writing. Go ahead, be brutally honest!

What happened was:

It happened because:

The result of this was:

Reflect

When you think you are being brutally honest with the truth, you are usually giving your interpretation of the event rather than the facts. Learning how to notice and manage your thoughts, both negative and positive ones, is an important part of building and regulating your epic self.

Go back to your "It happened because…" and come up with other possible reasons for what happened. Journal about it.

This week's practice was "Tell New Stories"
ASK YOURSELF DAILY: What went well today?
                       To get more of this I will . . .

WEEK TWO

Spot Your Thinking Traps

Learn

Your thoughts can be your greatest fans. Explanations can be helpful, like friends who look out for you and point out the positive. Other times your thoughts can push and pull you into directions that overwhelm you, or even keep you from seeing the truth. That's because of thinking biases. Consider the negativity bias. It makes you pay more attention to and remember negative information. Sometimes this is helpful, but you may also miss and forget the positive things that were happening.

Then there is the confirmation bias. It makes you pay more attention to evidence you are looking for, rather than being accurate and noticing what is actually there. Your mind can then jump to conclusions and may even catastrophize. Oh, no. What if _____ happens? You might feel anxious or even panicky, even when there is a positive alternative to your thought.

Grow

Learning to slow down and notice your thinking biases is an important feature of resilience. Say you see two friends of yours talking together. You wave and call out "Hello" to them, but neither of them responds to you. Worse yet, they both start laughing loudly. What do you think they are laughing about? It depends on your thinking biases and what mind traps you fall into as a result. You might make a connection between this event and an earlier one. Say you invited them to hang out with you and they turned you down. Your frame of reference could be negative, and it might make sense that they are laughing about you. You might think things like these:

- They did not respond to my invitation.
- They're trash-talking about me.
- They're laughing about me.
- They won't hang out with me.

Flourish
CHANGE A THOUGHT, CHANGE AN ACTION
Recognize that life is complicated, and your mind is often just trying to help. By neutralizing the negative background noise of thinking traps and activating positive thoughts, you can more often take new action. Practice challenging a negative assumption in four steps:

1. Remember that negative thoughts are stronger than positive ones. Then assume positive intent that doesn't feel so personal.

2. Remember that you will see the evidence you are looking for. Instead, look for evidence you may have missed.

3. Remember that you may ignore evidence that disagrees with your thoughts. Appreciate accurate alternative thoughts.

4. Remember that you may expect the worst and feel helpless. Instead, listen to your background noise and take action steps to get closer to what you want.

Reflect
It is not a thought itself, but what a thought means to you—your explanation and interpretation of a thought—that matters. Recall a troubling experience.

- What positive evidence could you have missed?
- Can you put the situation into perspective?
- What is the most likely (future) outcome?
- What different action might happen because of this more flexible thinking?

This week's practice was: "Spot Your Thinking Traps"
ASK YOURSELF DAILY: What went well today?
                        To get more of this I will . . .

WEEK THREE
Grow Your Mindset

Learn
Your mindset is a set of beliefs you have about yourself and the world. It guides your outlook, attitudes, and actions. If you tend toward the "fixed mindset" end of the spectrum, you believe that "smart" and "talented" are things you were born with—or without. From this point of view your success is a reflection of your fixed capabilities. You are working according to expectations.

If instead you have a growth mindset, you believe that how smart or capable you are is developed by a combination of what you think and do and feel. Whether fixed or growth, your mindset beliefs contribute to your willingness to act, the continued types of effort you put in, the strategies you use, and your explanations of the outcomes. With a growth mindset, there are many ways to get ahead.

Grow
If you lean towards a fixed mindset, you may wonder when your own talent won't be enough. When you don't meet a standard that has been set for you, your judger thoughts about yourself will explain to you that at some point your potential will be reached, perhaps today. You might tend to avoid challenges and ignore useful negative feedback. Eventually this can even lead to "what if?" anxiety and crippling self-doubt.

The good news? Mindsets are learned! This means you can learn a different one. If you tend towards a growth mindset, you will believe that you can help drive your success with a combination of your own efforts, support from others, and mindful focus. When you believe your potential is unknowable until you try, get feedback, and adjust your effort, you can treat performance as a valuable learning process rather than an evaluation.

Flourish

MY BEST FUTURE SELF

Imagine yourself five years from now. Imagine every positive outcome, including where you live, what you do each day, who you spend time with, and what you do for fun.

- Everything has gone right in your life.
- You have used your talents and abilities to grow and develop.
- You have considered constructive feedback and applied it to your goals and dreams.

1. What is the best future "you" like? What positive things do other people say about you?

2. Write about your best future self with lots of details and examples.

3. When you are finished, reread your story of the future you, and bask in how wonderful it feels.

Reflect

What is something that other people praise you for that you know you are good at because of your hard work, not just your talent?

This week's practice was: "Grow Your Mindset"
ASK YOURSELF DAILY: What went well today?
　　　　　　　　　　　To get more of this I will . . .

WEEK FOUR
Mind Your Mind Chatter

Learn
People, including you, are always having thoughts. This is called mind chatter. Most of this self-talk is explanations to ourselves of why we think things did, do, or will happen. The important thing to remember is that you can take control over whether you get stuck in a thought (are a judger) or are open to an alternative thought (are a learner).

A learner thought opens up new possibilities and builds on existing positive and optimistic thoughts. Strong judger thoughts, on the other hand, are often about threats and unfairness. Even when things actually are unfair, strong learner thoughts help refocus you on the opportunities that can come from incorporating feedback and focusing on strategies.

Grow
When you manage your mind chatter, you do more than just ignore it. You actively consider and change it. If you are having self-doubt, for example, remember a time in the past when you were at your best. Squash those thoughts that say you will never measure up or will always be at the end of the line. People who are good at optimistic and resilient thinking use their flexible thinking skills and say things like:

- "That's not true because…"
- "Another point of view could be…"
- "Most likely _____ will happen and I can do_____ to help."

Flourish
HOW DID I GET HERE? PRAISE THE PROCESS

Expand the evidence you are willing to consider by using process praise. Process praise is when effort and strategy, and not innate talent alone, are recognized as keys to improved performance. This approach helps build your growth mindset and prepare your thinking path for future performances. Give yourself a resilient thinking boost in three steps:

1. Think of a recent time when you needed to complete a difficult task and were successful.

2. Write down the steps you followed, and the reasons why you were a success.

3. Add specific details about what you contributed to the success by your actions, not your talent.

   What did you learn?

Reflect
How can you use positive comparisons to others to help you be more effective? (Hint: Think about people who inspire you.)

This week's practice was: "Mind Your Mind Chatter"
ASK YOURSELF DAILY: What went well today?
                          To get more of this I will . . .

WEEK FIVE
....
Build Hope

Learn
Say you really do want to succeed at a challenging task, but it seems unlikely to you. Should you give up without trying? A new challenge can happen at any point. Maybe you only see roadblocks to success. It might be like playing a game that keeps sending you back a space every time you have another turn. Should you stick with it? Sometimes it is difficult to imagine that things will work out well. Then it can be hard to be hopeful. You don't have to settle for failure, though. Instead, change the rules of the game!

Grow
It is important to face the truth that sometimes epic failures and disappointments can happen. You might not get exactly the outcome you desire. But building hope is not only possible; it can help you become more realistically optimistic. Thinking hopeful thoughts and feeling hopeful can help fuel the efforts you'll need to put into overcoming a challenge. Your thoughts, emotions, and actions can be used together as a powerful hope building tool. I call this the T-E-A Cycle.

Thoughts: Listen to the background noise of your thoughts and challenge the negative ones. Remember to mind your mind chatter.

Emotions: Notice your negative feelings as they shift when you challenge your negative thoughts. Focus on the motivation to do at least one thing necessary for success.

Actions: Find, create, or plan the first step on a pathway to possibility that will keep you feeling hopeful and moving ahead.

Flourish

MAKE ROOM FOR NOT KNOWING

Sometimes you will have an idea about how things might work out. You'll feel positive about the outcome. Other times you may not know what to expect and will feel unsure, worried, or anxious. Try making room for not knowing.

Recall a time when you accomplished something difficult. This was a time when you did not know for sure how things would turn out.

Then answer these questions:
1. How did you stay hopeful to successfully challenge the situation?

2. Can you remember any specific thoughts, emotions, and actions that helped keep you hopeful and that led to your success?

3. What made this outcome seem like a success to you?

Reflect

Sometimes only after some time has gone by are we able to realize that hope buoyed us during a challenge. How can you continue to make room for not knowing?

This week's practice was: "Build Hope"

ASK YOURSELF DAILY: What went well today?

To get more of this I will . . .

EXTEND YOUR OPTIMISM AND RESILIENCE
» Expect what's good
» Reframe what isn't

BE A RESILIENT THINKING S.T.A.R.

Use this worksheet over and over to help you move from a challenging situation to a revised action plan.

S: Situation _____

_____

T: Thoughts that might keep me stuck:_____

_____

A: Alternative thoughts:

"That's not true because _____"

"Another point of view could be _____"

"Most likely _____ will happen and I can do _____ to help."

R: Revised thoughts/Action plan _____

_____

_____

Here's what I did and what went well: _____

_____

_____

SECTION THREE
STRENGTHS

KEYS TO STRENGTHS

» Spot more of what's good about you.

» Develop new strengths.

You depend on your strengths to learn new skills, accomplish goals, nurture relationships, connect to communities, keep from overdoing things, and discover your meaning and purpose in the world.

To tap into the epic power of your strengths, you can learn how to use them in new ways.

Your character strengths contain a whole toolkit's worth of epic superpowers that you can learn to identify and then harness for your achievement and flourishing. Being able to identify and use your character strengths is linked with improved performance, and they are at work in all areas of life.

When you commit to discovering and developing your unique character strengths patterns, you can become happier, too. Researchers have found that people who know how to personalize using their strengths are also more resilient. Whether you are at home, school, activities, or work, being able to spot, develop, and connect with your strengths gives you important tools for enjoying your high points and managing your challenges.

Strengths Practices

WEEK ONE

Detect Your Strengths

WEEK TWO

Spot Strengths Heroes and Sidekicks

WEEK THREE

Manage Strengths Buttons

WEEK FOUR

Hitch Your Strengths to a Star

WEEK FIVE

Accomplish Together with Strengths

WEEK ONE
....

Detect Your Strengths

Learn

Imagine that when you put your sunglasses on, instead of just helping you adjust to bright light, they help adapt your perspective so that you see people, including yourself, through the lenses of strengths. Character strengths are more than just the nice things about a person. Spotting and focusing on strengths can help you progress more easily than tackling the challenge straight on or struggling to overcome weaknesses.

Consider the following clues to your strengths:

- What do you both enjoy and choose to do, whenever you can?
- What do other people say are the best things about you?
- What do you learn quickly, with what seems like little effort?
- What are the things about you that others can depend upon?

Grow

One of the best ways to flourish is to know and choose to use your character strengths. Your character strengths are your automatic response and your preferred, natural way to be yourself. When other people spot strength qualities in you and tell you about this, it feels good. Some of your strengths are like personality traits. Other strengths, like being brave or cautious, might pop up only when you need them. We all have a strengths signature. For instance, you may tend to be enthusiastic most of the time. Maybe you tend to persevere with difficult tasks. With practice you can adopt some new strengths.

Flourish
TAKE THE VIA STRENGTHS SURVEY

Here is one way to learn even more about strengths and discover yours.

1. Go to www.viacharacter.org
2. Register for the age-appropriate test: The VIA Youth Survey (10-17 years) or the VIA Signature Strengths Survey (18+).
3. After registering, begin the survey and respond to the statements.
4. Get your results.
5. Record all 24 of your VIA Character Strengths in a journal or by printing them out.

Reflect
Using the strengths numbered one to ten, choose the three that sound most like you. Say more about how you know. What is it about these three strengths that makes them feel right to you?

These strengths sound/feel/look like me because:

This week's practice was: "Detect Your Strengths"
ASK YOURSELF DAILY: What went well today?
To get more of this I will . . .

WEEK TWO
Spot Strengths Heroes and Sidekicks

Learn
When you took the Values in Action (VIA) Survey, you responded to actions that sound most like what you prefer or don't prefer in everyday situations. Now that you have been using your *Unleash Your Epic Self* workbook for several weeks, you can find language in it to describe your strengths in action. You can mine your *Flourish* activities and *Reflect* entries. Remember these three features of strengths that can make them easier to spot in yourself:

1. They are an automatic response.
2. They are your preferred way.
3. Other people who have the same exposure to an event or experience as you may respond differently because we all have unique combinations of strengths.

Grow
Another kind of strength is the sidekick. This strength is not a superpower by itself. You probably depend on it more than you realize, rather like the hero in a film depends on the supporting actor. When you team the sidekick with the strengths hero, you can get an even stronger team.

Here is an example. Say you have a teammate who is both very funny and energetic. You know this person has strengths of humor and zest. Sometimes this is what gives your team the positive edge it needs to win. Other times though, this player may overuse humor until it is more like sarcasm and demonstrate intensity when your team could use some calming and focusing.

If you have teamwork as a super strength, this kind of behavior could push your personal teamwork strengths button. A sidekick strength, like leadership, could help you guide your teammate to be more supportive of others, while social intelligence could help you know what to say and how to do that. Do you have a favorite movie with a sidekick? What strengths does the main character need that the sidekick offers? Your sidekick strengths regularly team up with your strengths heroes. Together these strengths teams can act as strengths superpowers.

Flourish

SIDEKICKS AND SUPERPOWERS

For this exercise, work with a partner. You will each need a list of your strengths.

1. Start by thinking of a recent time when you were at your best and using your strengths heroes. Briefly, write about it.

2. Now tell this story out loud to your partner who will listen for how you used your strengths heroes and sidekick strengths. When finished, allow your partner to spot the strengths they heard you using in your story.

3. Return the strengths-spotting favor. Ask your friend to tell you about a time when they were at their epic best. Now you become the listener. Be a strengths detective for your friend.

Reflect

This week notice how you use your dependable sidekick strengths to be at your best. How does it feel to use different combinations of strengths?

This week's practice was: "Spot Strengths Heroes and Sidekicks"

ASK YOURSELF DAILY: What went well today?
                      To get more of this I will . . .

WEEK THREE
Manage Strengths Buttons

Learn
It can be hard to work against your strengths. They are your automatic response and feel right. In this way, honest people may find it hard to tell even a harmless untruth, and forgiving people may let others hurt them over and over. These are examples of overdoing it with a strength. The reverse, underusing a strength, can also happen. For instance, you may struggle to complete tasks. Some self-regulation and perseverance strengths would help, but maybe they are hard for you.

Grow
People also have "strengths buttons." That's why sometimes you'll have a strong reaction when your strengths are challenged or feel violated by someone else. Strengths buttons get pushed when other people's strengths are either different from or in conflict with your own. Imagine that you observe someone who shows ungrateful behavior. Because you might automatically expect them to show the thanks that you would in a similar situation, you may feel a strong judger reaction toward the person. This could happen if gratitude comes easily to you. After the button for your well-developed strength is pushed, you may react with even more strong feelings and behaviors.

Since your relationships with others depend on balancing your needs and wants with those of the other person, knowing how to manage these moments when your strengths buttons have been pushed can make a big difference. You can prevent overreacting by observing your mind chatter when you are having a strengths moment. Feeling disgusted? Angry? Afraid? Any time you react with a strong negative emotion and judger thoughts, it is worth asking yourself if a strengths button has been pushed.

Flourish

HAVING A MOMENT

Do you keep track of daily hassles and aggravation? Instead of feeling angry, worried, or sad, analyze them through a strengths lens. Try this:

1. Go back to your VIA Survey results. Start with the three most automatic strengths. Now think of an example of a time in the past few days when you felt like someone else really aggravated you.

2. Remember that the bigger the superpower, the bigger the strengths button moment. What are your superpower strengths buttons? What about this situation pushed them?

3. Did it feel as if the other person was annoying you on purpose? Maybe they were using their strengths, too. What strengths that you did not choose as your superpowers would make it easier for you to reframe the experience?

Reflect

Sometimes other people become frustrated with you when they think you need to show more of certain strengths. It can sound like, **"You're so impulsive!"** (maybe not showing self-regulation) or **"You give up so easily!"** (maybe not showing perseverance). What strengths do you sometimes wish were easier for you? What can you say to someone who criticizes your strengths challenges?

This week's practice was: "Manage Strengths Buttons"
ASK YOURSELF DAILY: What went well today?
                     To get more of this I will . . .

WEEK FOUR
Hitch Your Strengths to a Star

Learn
Your success and well-being benefit from the ways you spot and manage your own strengths. Sometimes you will want to change them up, depending on different expectations of culture, circumstances, and people.

You now have these strengths tools in your toolkit:

- Strengths Heroes: Make it easier to be at your best
- Sidekick Strengths: Help strengths heroes be superheroes
- Strengths Buttons: When situations push these, you can notice and manage "having a moment"

You also have challenge strengths. They are the easily overused or underused ones that work better when hitched to a star. For instance, if fairness is important to you, you might notice that you are having an "unfairness" moment when things don't go your way. Maybe it rained on your special weekend, your favorite restaurant was closed when you finally had time to go there, or you felt unjustly overworked. Blame and anger can boil over at these moments.

Grow
When life hands you challenges, you can learn to flexibly blend and connect your strengths with each other. If you have *modesty* as a strength it can be difficult to stick up for yourself. An unfairness moment could leave you simmering with anger. Hitching *perspective* to *fairness* can help you realize that no one wanted you to have to go without your favorite things or feel overwhelmed. For example, you can reschedule when the weather is better, or when the restaurant is open. By hitching *honesty* to *modesty*, it can become easier to explain how you really feel, and what you really want.

Flourish
DEVELOP YOUR STRENGTHS

Read this quotation and then respond to the questions below:

"The content of your character is your choice. Day by day, what you choose, what you think, and what you do is who you become."
~Marcus Aurelius: Stoic Philosopher, Roman Emperor

1. Choose strengths that you wish came more easily to you.
2. Write what you think the benefits will be of developing these strengths.
3. What will you do to hitch your challenge strengths to a star one?

Reflect
What kind of person would you like to become one year from today? Which of your character strengths will energize you on that journey?

This week's practice was:
"Hitch Your Strengths to a Star"
ASK YOURSELF DAILY: What went well today?
To get more of this I will . . .

WEEK FIVE

Accomplish Together with Strengths

Learn
One of the most fascinating things about strengths is that a group or organization has its own strengths profile. Often without realizing it, people give each other informal feedback about their strengths. Some people may feel like they fit right in because they share values, identity, and behaviors with the group norms.

Other people may feel marginalized and think that their particular strengths are less valued than the general group's. Strengths are good things about people by definition. When all kinds of strengths are valued, you will find new ways to think about how you and others can contribute to the meaning, purpose, and productivity of your family, friends, or work group.

Grow
Do you compliment your friends, family, and work colleagues by describing the character strengths you see them using? Sometimes people think that being critical of others makes them sound smart. Scientists have found, though, that building on people's strengths—what they do right and developing them—creates more benefit than focusing on their weaknesses—what they do wrong—and trying to correct them. Can you think of new ways to use strengths?

Another way of hitching strengths to a star happens when a group knows each other's strengths and can intentionally use them together in new ways. This in turn can help to forge stronger team bonds and problem-solving. Using strengths-based feedback between peers and among teammates can also create positive feedback loops that support both individual and team success.

Flourish

GROUP STRENGTHS GALLERY

This is a group activity. You will need a blank space like a wall or white board, sticky notes, and pens. Do this activity with family, friends, and work colleagues. More people means more strengths to share! Start by reading the first four steps and then following them:

What to do:
1. Everyone will take the VIA Strengths Survey, like you did, here: www.viacharacter.org.
2. Write each one of the 24 strengths on a separate sticky note. Spread them around on a blank space such as a wall or white board.
3. Give each person five sticky notes. Have everyone write their name on each of their sticky notes, along with one of their top strengths.
4. Each person will match their five sticky notes to one of the strengths on the wall or board.

Next, ask these questions:
1. What are the top strengths of your group?
2. Who shares your strengths? Did you expect this?
3. Are there any strengths that no one in your group chose?

Reflect

- If your group needed more of a strength that doesn't come easily to anyone, where could it come from?
- How can using strengths together help people accomplish more?

This week's practice was:
"Accomplish Together with Strengths"
ASK YOURSELF DAILY: What went well today?
To get more of this I will . .

EXTEND YOUR STRENGTHS
» Get more of what's good about you
» Develop new strengths

STRENGTHS STRETCH FOR TEAMS

Many times in life you will be on a team working toward shared goals. This happens in school or at work, as well as in family and friend groups. Your group may need strengths that are a stretch.

Imagine that you are in a group of four. One person has strong self-regulation. Other strengths in your group may include social intelligence, leadership, and creativity. Think beyond the strongest individual performer. What are the top strengths of each of your group members? (Hint: They can all take the VIA Strengths Survey).

Everyone can give a lift to others who may need a strength that does not come easily to them. How can each group member contribute their capabilities so that others can hitch their strengths to a star strength and get the stretch the group needs? What strengths can be pulled up when they are attached to Star Strengths?

Our group needs a lift for these strengths: _____

_____

_____

Here's how we hitched our strengths to star strengths within our group.

_____

_____

SECTION FOUR:
EMOTIONAL INTELLIGENCE

KEYS TO EMOTIONAL INTELLIGENCE
» Develop solid relationships.
» Be grateful, forgiving, and kind.

Everyone likes to get presents. A gift does not need to be in a box with a ribbon, though. When someone shows you kindness, especially when you are feeling down, this is also a gift. In your everyday life, you depend on having other people respond to your needs and wants this way. When you have a strong network of supportive friends and family, you know you matter to someone besides yourself. This connection to other people builds positivity, optimism, and resilience. Experiencing genuine gratitude toward the people in your life also discourages you from doing things that would be destructive to your relationships.

Positive friendships in particular help to decrease stress and anxiety and can even reduce the risk of depression. People with solid friendships tend to live longer, happier, healthier lives. When you build a genuine connection with someone, you're more likely to have a supportive friend with you during the inevitable rough patches in life. This helps you to keep calm, feel supported, and work through your challenges while you explore unexpected chances to use your strengths in new ways.

Would you like to be in a positive mood more often and increase your well-being? Build your self-awareness and curiosity, reach out to others with generosity, let go of grudges with forgiveness, and learn how to apologize with sincerity.

Emotional Intelligence Practices

WEEK ONE
Practice Self-Compassion

WEEK TWO
Tell Me More

WEEK THREE
Be Emotionally Contagious

WEEK FOUR
Commit Acts of Kindness

WEEK FIVE
Give Up on Grudges

WEEK ONE:
Practice Self-Compassion

Learn
Self-compassion is a way to offer yourself the same care, understanding, and support you would offer others who are struggling. Fortunately, you can learn to treat yourself with the same combination of honest care and encouragement that you would use with a friend. When you think both accurate and kind thoughts about yourself, you are giving yourself permission to be the whole, imperfect person everyone is. However, this doesn't mean that you will stop striving to be your very best. Instead it means you can face failures with acceptance, responsibility, and new direction, but without shaming criticism. This is essential for continued effort.

Grow
Everyone fails sometimes. What could you say to a friend who worried about how they measured up while working toward a goal? First of all, you could comfort them. Then you could help them to see their strengths in what went well, and steer them away from negatively comparing themselves to others. Helping them think of failures and disappointments as learning experiences can help, too. Finally, you could help them take the next steps toward success. Showing compassion, empathy, and support are marks of a good friend.

Flourish
SELF-COMPASSION EXERCISE

You can be a good friend to yourself. Here's how:

1. Think of something you have struggled with lately. Have you had judger thoughts about this struggle? Think about how you would treat a friend with the same challenge. How will you show yourself compassion, empathy, and support?

2. Now encourage your struggling self to try, maybe in a new way. Be sure to notice what has gone well, calm your mind chatter, and focus on your strengths. What can you do next? Write your thoughts.

Reflect
Kindness is a powerful antidote to fear. You might hear your worry in words like "What if I..." or "I'll never...". Those are worry signals in your mind chatter. When you hear worry signals, it is a reminder to use self-compassion. Are there times when you are more likely to judge yourself? When can you practice self-compassion?

This week's practice was: "Practice Self-Compassion"
ASK YOURSELF DAILY: What went well today?
                To get more of this I will . . .

WEEK TWO

Tell Me More

Learn
You know how important it is to have self-compassion. Showing compassion and interest in others is important, too. One way to show others that you care is by using the "Tell Me More" response. You might already use this when someone else shares good news. Research consistently shows that people feel cared for and more connected to others when a listener responds in a way that gets the person who is sharing good news to tell even more about the event.

Grow
Using the Tell Me More response style predicts the positive strength of a relationship. You can use it with anyone, and both of you will gain well-being benefits. Researchers have found that people use four key styles of responding to the good news of another person. Imagine that an excited friend has just told you that they've been offered a new position. They have worked hard for this recognition. Think about how you could respond to them:

"Tell me more."
(Keeps the conversation going! Lets the person know you are interested!)

"That's great."
(Polite but ends the conversation.)

"You'll be sorry. What if you _____?"
(Points out why the good news might be bad. Makes you sound critical.)

"Check out my new shoes."
(Shows you are off-topic. Makes you seem self-interested.)

Flourish
TELL ME MORE

To get your social-emotional boost from the Tell Me More style of responding, you need to make it both active (You're really responding to what the other person said) and constructive (You're not shooting them down by your response). You will be listening with thoughtful attention and using genuine curiosity to ask questions so they will want to share even more with you. That's how connection happens.

Practice this strategy in two steps:
1. **Practice with a friend.** Take turns sharing something good that happened to you recently. Let your friend share first. It doesn't need to be a giant win. It is your turn to listen and ask questions. Keep them talking and sharing about the event. Be genuinely interested and curious.

   You can ask things like:
   - And then what happened?
   - What was that like?
   - What was the best part?

2. **Switch roles.** Now it's your turn to share. If you get stuck, remember that you have lots of "What Went Well" entries right here in your workbook. Tell a good news story to your friend. They need to keep you talking, too.

Reflect
How did that go? What was it like to encourage someone else to feel comfortable to talk because you are actively listening and responding? What could make it even better?

This week's practice was: "Tell Me More"
ASK YOURSELF DAILY: What went well today?
To get more of this I will . . .

WEEK THREE
Be Emotionally Contagious

Learn

If you want to improve your well-being, one way is to be more in charge of your choice of companions. How do you choose to spend your social time? Do you mostly choose to be with happy and high-performing friends? Social contagion is the tendency for your emotions and behaviors to spread throughout your social network. In this way, happy, successful people will tend to have happy, successful friends. It also works in reverse. Since negative emotions and behaviors also spread, a group of people who have problems like excessive drinking, smoking, or bullying can spread those behaviors like germs. Yuck.

Grow

Sometimes what you need is a good laugh. Negative thoughts and emotions release stress hormones into the body. You can counteract them with some belly laughter. Laughing, even when you have to pretend to start with, is a well-being builder. Laughter triggers hormones that work to reverse the effects of stress, and they also help you to think in new ways. This lets you be ready to learn and achieve. You can even spread happiness with a group laughter practice. Remember that positive emotions are contagious.

You don't need to ignore unhappy people. In fact, you can spread your positivity to them. Researchers have found that people whose friends have strong well-being are much less likely to become depressed compared to those with emotionally unhealthy friends. People suffering from depression often withdraw from friends. If you are depressed, your emotionally healthy friends can spread some of their happiness to you. Also, keep going to your counselor, social club, school, or work, even when you feel down. You can catch the happier bug there. Remember to notice even small things that are going well. And if you know someone who is sad, use the power of social contagion to share your well-being.

Flourish
BELLY LAUGHING

Here is a chance to be a little bit silly with yourself and a friend.

1. Lie on your back with your palms facing up. Close your eyes.
2. Laugh as hard as you can for no particular reason, pulling the belly in when you ha, ha, ha. Try to do this for a whole minute.
3. Experiment and have fun with laughing practice. What kinds of laughter did you notice? How do you feel after laughing just for fun?

Reflect
Some people enjoy being like the sun, at the center of everything. Other people like to be a planet orbiting, as part of a group. Where are you most comfortable in your social network? What emotional contagion do you bring to the groups you are part of?

This week's practice was: "Be Emotionally Contagious"
ASK YOURSELF DAILY: What went well today?
                        To get more of this I will . . .

WEEK FOUR
Commit Acts of Kindness

Learn
Kindness to others results in what researchers call the "Helper's High". It's the result of brain chemicals called endorphins. These are the same chemicals as the ones released when you engage in strenuous exercise. They make you feel proud, uplifted, and hopeful.

When you are generous to others, you are also more likely to be actively involved in your local community. The kindness you share brings positivity to others and deepens your connection to them. This releases the feel-good brain chemical called oxytocin. It makes you feel more socially bonded and want to be even more generous.

Grow
Being kind to others brings well-being benefits to you. Voluntarily giving leads to happier, healthier, longer lives. Kindness counteracts stress hormones and can successfully decrease physical reactivity. Committing acts of kindness also contributes to making you feel calmer and more optimistic. Over time, kindness can even lower your risk of anxiety and depression. Remember that emotions are contagious. Kindness brings meaning and purpose to life. As a result you are more likely to feel successful. Because of your positive connections to others, you'll feel better about yourself, too.

Flourish
RANDOM ACTS OF KINDNESS

Start with Random Acts of Kindness. These are ones where you are not repaying or reciprocating for a kindness you have received. You are giving because you want to. Use your own social awareness to help you notice what other people might need, and add some creativity to come up with unique ideas. Even if you do not know a person you help, you will benefit from being kinder.

Try one of these:
- **Anonymous method**
  You may not know the person you help but will see their reaction. Examples are paying for the person ahead in the drive-thru lane, letting someone go ahead of you in line, complimenting a stranger, or holding the door open for someone else. I use this method when I take my therapy dog to visit nursing home and memory care center residents who we help but do not know.

- **Invisible method**
  Only you will know that you have done a kind thing, and you will not know whom you help. Examples are putting money in a vending machine, giving blood if you are able, taking grocery gift cards to a food pantry. I use this approach when I leave my favorite gently used picture books in a community free library.

1. How will you be kind? Anonymous or Invisible?
2. Where will you be kind? Home, School, Work, Community?
3. Can you perform at least five acts of kindness, one per day this week?

Reflect

What kind things did you do? Did you see the ones you helped? What would you like to do again? What would make your Random Acts of Kindness even better?

This week's practice was: "Commit Acts of Kindness"
ASK YOURSELF DAILY: What went well today?
                      To get more of this I will . . .

WEEK FIVE

Give Up on Grudges

Learn

Are you holding a grudge? Carrying a grudge can make it difficult to look ahead in a relationship. Until you begin to forgive you may struggle to have the desire to move on. Forgiveness is not the same as pretending that a wrong is right, and it can be very challenging since you may need to give up the sense that you have been wronged or cheated. Forgiveness happens in small stages. You give up your anger and negative judgment about the person who unjustly hurt you. Guess what? Even if you no longer trust the other person, you can still forgive them. When you forgive someone, you aren't doing it for the other person. You are doing it for yourself. You don't have to forget that your rights have been violated. If you want, you can still work toward having the other person mend fences with you.

Grow

When you retain resentment you will have higher levels of negative emotions. You're more likely to feel a lack of personal control and have spikes in physical and emotional stress. No one wants that. Over time a "madness meal" feeds both stress hormones and hostility. This can lead to serious illnesses like cardiovascular disease and immune system problems. By forgiving though, you will stop feeding the negativity monsters of anger, bitterness, hatred, and resentment. You'll show others that you don't hold grudges and are open to rebuilding trust, the foundation of continuing relationships. When you reduce resentment, you can also have higher self-worth, greater happiness, and lower physical reactivity. You can feel both physically and emotionally lighter.

Flourish

BUILD FORGIVENESS MUSCLE

The key to becoming more forgiving is to start small. Instead of trying to forgive a big injustice, begin your practice with a slight just a bit bigger than something that would be easy to let go of. So treat it more like a random act of kindness than a peace treaty with enemy countries! Try one of these:

1. Imagine that you are standing at the starting line for a sprint. The first time you run you are wearing a backpack with three heavy stones that represent grudges you have been carrying. The second time you run you leave the backpack on the sidelines. Which race is better/faster/more fun? What grudges did you leave on the sidelines?

2. Choose three grudges you have been carrying. Write them on three separate small pieces of paper. Cross them out. Crumple them up. One at a time, put them on your palm and with a big breath blow them away, into the paper trash. You don't need them. Imagine them gone forever.

3. For bigger grudges use your imagination and the perspective strength to help you. Remember to hitch it to a star strength if it is not one of your superpowers. Which strengths will you try?

Keep practicing this week and beyond. Which approach will you try?

Reflect

Sometimes the grudges we carry are about actual slights. How can you benefit by giving up your anger? What can you say to your mind chatter to be able to let the grudge go?

This week's practice was: "Give Up on Grudges"
ASK YOURSELF DAILY: What went well today?
                       To get more of this I will . . .

EXTEND YOUR EMOTIONAL INTELLIGENCE
» Develop solid relationships
» Be grateful, forgiving and kind

THE ASKING SCRIPT

Good relationships depend on solid communication. Knowing how to ask without sounding judgmental is a skill you can learn and practice for a lifetime.

Before you get started...here's what not to say:
What is wrong with you? Why don't you just . . .? I just need you to . . .

Remember you are asking, not telling (It sounds bossy) or pointing out what they did wrong (It sounds judgy), or saying why it ought to be easy (It sounds shaming).

Get started like this:
1. Know what you want the other person to do: I want them to _____
2. Be sure it is **R.A.P.**
   - Reasonable because_____
   - Actionable because_____
   - Practical because_____

Fill in these sentence starters:
1. I noticed that . . .
   (you wore my new shirt without asking)

2. I feel . . .
   (sad and angry because it was a gift and I did not get to wear it yet)

3. I want you to . . .
   (leave my things alone unless I say it's ok)

4. Will you . . .
   (ask me before you use my things)

What went well?
Reflect the other person's strengths back to them by offering prompt, positive praise.

"Thank you for _____. I love the way you _____."

SECTION FIVE:
DECISION MAKING AND CHANGE

KEYS TO DECISION MAKING AND CHANGE
» Desire what's good.
» Manage obstacles to success.

Do you blame "circumstances" like the weather or other people for your inability to change? You can nearly always change your response and attention to events. That's an important ability, since no matter how old you are, you have a lifetime of decisions to make. All decisions have outcomes. Every action that you take or avoid is a choice, even when you are not consciously aware of this happening. In order for your choices to become intentional and useful time-saving habits that free you to experience new learning, you need to stay focused on what is good and useful in your life.

Making choices is complicated by overpowering emotions, the background noise of social pressure, and short-term gain found in avoidance. Sometimes you will face challenges where change will become necessary. Three things are the foundation of change: attention, habit, and will. In other words, you need to notice what you are doing in order to stop doing it so much; you need to develop an alternate and more effective habit; and you need to develop staying power. This can mean using "won't" as opposed to "will" power.

Chances are that you have made some choices you regret. People grow by learning lessons about what already went well, or didn't, and from trying differently next time. Imagine the pathways you can maneuver on as you choose and learn from your actions. A pathway that supports responsible personal boundaries can help prevent you from losing your way on your well-being journey. Better choices are built on strengths, self-awareness, and habits.

Decision Making and Change Practices

WEEK ONE

Be Your Own Boss

WEEK TWO

Train and Care for Your Elephant

WEEK THREE

Cue New Habits

WEEK FOUR

If This, Then That

WEEK FIVE

Manage Procrastination

WEEK ONE

Be Your Own Boss

Learn

Have you ever wished you could be your own boss? Many people vacillate between wanting someone else to tell them exactly what to do versus dreaming of being in charge of their own life and work. Sometimes this wish comes from feelings of resentment that may come up when they have too much responsibility without enough freedom. Other times it happens when people see opportunities for improvement that no one else seems to care about. What could it be like if you were in charge of you?

Bosses have workers, so being the boss of you will mean you are also a worker. If you are the boss, your workers will need at least some direction and reassurance to keep moving ahead if they feel overwhelmed, angry, or fearful. Sometimes workers are sick, want time off, or think they deserve to be paid more for their work. How will you manage these typical worker concerns if you are in charge of yourself? This is something that you can easily try in your imagination before you jump into doing it for real.

Grow

Before you can be the boss, you will want to know what you want from your workers. Chances are you will want them to have well-developed skills for the job and to be consistent and adaptable. You will want them to demonstrate self-regulation in all areas of their work, including punctuality, diligence, teamwork skills, and the ability to delay gratification. You will want them to have enough optimism to keep projects from becoming stalled from lack of action, plus persistence so that projects are completed.

Flourish

YOU ARE THE BOSS

As the boss you must be self-directed. That means no one will be explicitly telling you just what to do or when to do it. Great, you may be thinking. Now I can sleep in! However, as the boss of you, you'll need to be able to answer many questions about how to meet the minimum standards required for keeping the business of you on track. What are your answers to these questions?

- What does the business of you produce?
- What skills are required of the workers? How do they get even better at their work?
- What if workers slack off? Does the boss have management approaches for keeping workers engaged?
- What constraints must be managed for available resources, time, and money?
- How will you measure worker success?
- Can you fire yourself? Whether yes or no, how will you keep the business of you on track?

Reflect

What strengths heroes and sidekicks do you bring to the role of being your own boss? What is the most appealing part of being in charge of yourself?

This week's practice was: "Be Your Own Boss"
ASK YOURSELF DAILY: What went well today?
To get more of this I will . . .

WEEK TWO
Train and Care for Your Elephant

Learn
Look back at last week's practice about being the boss of you. What was on your to-do list? Did you give yourself lots of time off? A big pay hike? A posh office space? If so, you gave your emotional self a positivity boost. One of my favorite teachers told us to imagine that our emotional self is like an elephant. Huge and powerful, it is guided by fears and desires more than by hopes and plans. The emotional elephant can struggle to control its behavior and may stray from the positive choice path. That's why every elephant needs a guide or rider. This is the tiny but logical boss (you!) who cues it and plans elephant rewards for taking the right actions. The rider also anticipates what is ahead on the pathway and stays focused on the end goal by managing mind chatter. Emotional elephants definitely need help with that.

Grow
Because the emotional elephant in you is stronger than the logical rider, the rider needs to build powerful logic and planning skills. When the rider/elephant pair is working well together, they are motivated to stick to the positive choice path. Their thoughts, emotions, and actions move them closer to success. Three things are particularly helpful for keeping your emotional elephant on track. First, because the elephant is huge and reactive, it will help to set strong elephant management limits or rules in advance. Also, you'll want to clear the pathway of distractions that can take the elephant off track when it is worried, angry, or sad, and wants to escape, push back, or withdraw from the pathway. Finally, your emotional elephant can be reminded with subtle cues that take advantage of logic, planning, and skills.

Flourish

CONSISTENT PATHWAYS/LIMITED CHOICES

Think about a time this week when you really did not want to do what was expected of you. What was it? How did you react? Did you avoid it altogether? Were you able to turn your emotional elephant around?

Now answer the following questions to imagine a less effort-filled approach to regulating your emotions:

- What distractions does your emotional elephant seek when you are faced with tasks that you do not prefer? (Think food, phone, fun...)
- What are some good rules or choice limits for times when distractions are hard to resist? (Think: First work, then play...)
- What are good reminders for you so your emotional elephant knows what is expected instead of waiting to be called out? (Think planner, reminders, rewards for success...)

Reflect

How is the rider a kind of boss? What are your rider's top skills for managing your emotional elephant? What skills could you develop even more?

This week's practice was:
"Train and Care for Your Elephant"
ASK YOURSELF DAILY: What went well today?
                      To get more of this I will . . .

WEEK THREE
Cue New Habits

Learn
Just trying harder is not enough to create a habit. Habits require emotional motivation that links your behavior to your goal. Before trying to make a new habit, learn what your emotional elephant needs for it to face a challenge. Powerful positive emotions are the reward of a job well done. Elephants like snacks, so give yourself little emotional rewards along the pathway to stay motivated to continue, especially when the work is challenging. Emotional rewards are not the same as being given something like money or a prize for a strong performance. They aren't bribes, either. Instead, think of what your emotional elephant needs to stick to the path. No matter how many big, angry, fearful, or sad feelings you have, use your rider to tell new stories that calm, focus, and reassure your emotional elephant.

Grow
Why should you make new habits? One reason is that habits make behaviors more automatic, so they are time savers. Time is something we all want more of! Establishing habits is easiest when you want to make a behavior automatic, can set up a pathway with limited distractions, and are willing to accept small emotional rewards to keep you moving along. It can help you to anticipate success and savor the future. Placing sensory cues along the pathway to your goal is one way to remind you of how good you'll feel when your goal has been met. Since all rewards cause you to react with emotions, make your cues positive ones rather than punishments. Choose cues that give you bite-sized bits of pride, interest, or inspiration. This will encourage your emotional elephant when it is feeling more energy for resisting the work than focused direction for practicing the habit.

Flourish

HABIT FORMING

What is a habit you have that you need to replace in order to break it? It is easier to make a new habit than to change an old one. Here is how:

- Disrupt an old habit you find hard to end by cueing yourself for new positive action. Say you want to make a habit of making your bed each day. As much as you say you want to do this, you don't follow through. That's because the old habit of not making the bed still exists.
- Rather than try to break it, replace it with something else that you want to do more. Use the new thing as your cue. If you want to run first, by leaving your shoes in the doorway, your emotional self would be reminded like this: Want to take a run? Make your bed first!

Now it's time for you to cue a new habit:
1. What is the new habit you want to establish?
2. What existing habit has parts of your cue built in, like the shoes above?
3. How will you set up your routine to cue you for your new habit?

Reflect

A successful habit gets you more of something that you want. What are some habits you would like to change? Maybe you stay in bed after the alarm goes off, or you leave things at home that you need for work, school, or training. Maybe you interrupt when others are speaking, or complain about people behind their back. Make a list of any habits you wish you did not have.

This week's practice was: "Cue New Habits"
ASK YOURSELF DAILY: What went well today?
                                        To get more of this I will . . .

WEEK FOUR
....
If This, Then That

Learn
You learned earlier that your rider is great at logic and can use this ability to guide your emotional elephant. When things seem fine or at least good enough, though, there is little to no motivation to make them different. You may even find that other people who suggest change to you seem overly critical, even when their feedback is on target! Sometimes your rider will see a need for change, but your emotional elephant won't feel that there is a problem to address. In order to change for good, the rider needs to help the elephant to want to change. In other words, change has to seem appealing and necessary.

Grow
Scientists who study habit change have found that there are several steps involved in the change process. The words in *italics* are thoughts, and in parentheses are what the person is motivated to do or not. The steps go like this:

1. *That's your problem.*
   (No motivation to change)

2. *It's my problem and I'll get around to fixing it.*
   (Motivation/No plan to change)

3. *It's my problem and this is my plan for fixing it.*
   (Motivation and a plan, but no work)

4. *I'm actively working on my problem.*
   (Motivation/Plan/Action)

5. *My behavior is a habit.*
   (Motivation to continue)

Do you see that owning the problem, making a plan, and taking action are keys to a motivated solution?

Flourish

IF THIS —>THEN THAT

Remember that making changes can be hard. Everyone wants to slack off now and then. When the present feels heavy and discouraging, you need to have the will to stick with a challenge.

Make off-track times easier by planning ahead for when you may have more "won't power" than willpower.

1. Pay attention to things that distract you from forming new habits. Make a list of them.

2. Now reframe these distractions by writing IF in front of each distraction and THEN before a solution that will get you back on track, like this:

If —>	Then...
If I want to keep taking breaks	**then** I will set a timer.

Reflect

What are the three to five most common ways that you are often distracted? What will you plan so that instead of giving yourself permission to be off track, say you just forgot, or blame circumstances beyond your control, you can actually be in charge?

This week's practice was: "If This, Then That"

ASK YOURSELF DAILY: What went well today?

To get more of this I will . . .

WEEK FIVE
Manage Procrastination

Learn
Here is some review: Habits provide comfort and reassurance by presenting you with a familiar situation. To start a habit, you need a cue. Leaving your sneakers by the bedside where you will see them first thing can be a cue to exercise. You also need a reward. Rewards are emotional, not tangible. You stick with a habit because of how it makes you feel (think: elephant snacks), and eventually, that reward will also help you get something else that you want: rider success. Will you be happier? Will you be more connected to your friends? What will you gain from the consistent habit, beyond greater efficiency?

Grow
Of course, no good comes from a habit that you do not act on. In last week's practice you learned the importance of having a strategy for times when you lack the motivation to work on change. Procrastination, which you probably think is a productivity problem, is often more about managing your mood. Recognizing how you are feeling can be another way to help get you motivated. Procrastination often helps you use the anxiety of the last minute to get going. Everyone has a different sweet spot for this. You may feel a bit nervous as a deadline approaches, or you may feel absolute panic. Use procrastination for good by managing time and difficulty.

Flourish

SMALLER SOONER, LARGER LATER

When you have either lots of time to get something done, or it seems like an easy task, your motivation may be low. The opposite scenario, a short amount of time or a very difficult task, can lead to anxiety.

Start with these five ways to help manage procrastination:

1. Listen to your background noise. Get into your best personal sweet spot by moving into neutral, feeling neither bored nor panicky about the task.

2. Slipping toward boredom? Bump up your due date. Make an easier task more challenging by shrinking the time available to complete it.

3. Instead of putting off a task, plan something fun right before the last minute that you would not want to miss. Get your work done beforehand. Celebrate!

4. When you have a very challenging task, break it up into smaller parts that are less difficult individually.

5. If it is possible to complete parts of a task out of order, choose the part you like best to start your work. You'll build both positive emotion and momentum this way.

Reflect

What does it mean to make the last minute happen sooner? When is this a good idea? What did you move into the sweet spot, and how did you do it?

This week's practice was: "Manage Procrastination"
ASK YOURSELF DAILY: What went well today?
                             To get more of this I will . . .

EXTEND YOUR DECISION MAKING AND CHANGE
» Desire what's good
» Manage obstacles to success

5-10-50 DECISION MAKING

Sometimes people get stuck making decisions. It can be hard to imagine the impacts of a decision at several future times. Use 5-10-50 Decision Making any time you want to understand what it will be like to manage through a range of possible impacts that might play out over time. You can also use this to help you consider changing a habit or creating a new one. It works best with *either this/or this* choices.

I need to make a decision to _____ Or _____	Imagine possibilities over time: X time from now, this is most likely
What will happen if I make this decision? (Impact in days)	5 days from now _____ 10 days from now _____ 50 days from now _____
What will happen if I make this decision? (Impact in weeks)	5 weeks from now _____ 10 weeks from now _____ 50 weeks from now _____
What will happen if I make this decision? (Impact in years)	5 years from now _____ 10 years from now _____ 50 years from now _____
My actual decision:	Why I chose it:

SECTION SIX:
GOAL SETTING, GRIT, AND GROWTH MINDSET

KEYS TO GOAL SETTING, GRIT, AND GROWTH MINDSET
» Plan for and stick with what's good.
» Use the power of YET.

All of us have goals of some kind that will take focus, long-term hard work, and resilience. You have learned so far in your *Unleash Your Epic Self* workbook that Positivity is the foundation of success; Optimism keeps you willing to push ahead while Resilience gives you the ability to bounce back when things do not go as planned; Strengths can be harnessed to become your sidekicks and superpowers; Emotional Intelligence keeps you self-aware, more open to working with others, and able to be both grateful and forgiving; Decision Making and Change skills help you start and keep new habits and manage procrastination.

In this section you will practice Goal Setting. When connected to the attitudes and behaviors of Grit and a Growth Mindset, this can lead to new successes. Maintaining focus and energy for achieving goals can be difficult. It can even make you feel less happy some days. You may question why you try so hard when the path to success can include injury, disappointment, and embarrassment. It's worth the struggle, because achieving challenging goals can feel amazing. You will be full of many positive emotions, including joy, pride, awe, and even relief. Phew!

If your success story happens while you are part of a group or team, these experiences with other people can lead to personal and community connection. When you face challenges with others who are close to you, such as friends, family, and colleagues, you create shared success stories, strengthen your relationships, and build a sense that your lives together matter.

Goal Setting, Grit, and Growth Mindset Practices

WEEK ONE
Follow the Three Rules for Adulting

WEEK TWO
Just Get Started Daily

WEEK THREE
Make a Growth Mindset Goal Plan

WEEK FOUR
Reward Small Wins Regularly

WEEK FIVE
Be Gritty and Accountable

WEEK ONE

Follow the Three Rules for Adulting

Learn
When you intend to do something, do you leave a lot of latitude for *not* doing it? You might. Intending to do something implies that you probably will do it. It could sound like, "I'll probably do it this week." "I'll probably get around to it later." If you really want to practice powerful goal-setting and achievement behaviors, whether for big or small objectives, research shows that intentions will not help. That's because there is often a gap between your intention and your action. Every intention has the "p" word embedded in it. That word is *probably*, which leaves room for "probably not".

Grow
Probably is a thought and emotion barrier that must be overcome in order for you to take action. To stick with behaviors that lead to goal achievement, remember that taking distractions away from your emotional elephant, making the last minute happen sooner, and having a backup plan are keys to creating a new habit. Taking advantage of your good habits can lead to greater consistency and save time when you want to accomplish a goal.

Flourish

MASTER THE THREE RULES FOR ADULTING

Do you have a goal you'd like to achieve? The Three Rules for Adulting are a 1-2-3 action cycle that will help you take advantage of planning, assessing, and recalibrating your goal-directed behaviors. Let's get started!

Write your goal here: _____

Then ask yourself:

- Do I have the skills I need? Are new skills part of my goal?
- Can I organize my schedule around the goal?
- Can I commit to necessary practice?

Now follow the Three Rules for Adulting:
Rule #1: Assign yourself the **time and kind of work you will do to work on this goal.**

1. Plan ahead with the end in mind, working backwards from the desired end
2. Break down large tasks into practical, measurable, actionable steps
3. Estimate time and prioritize activities in a planner, calendar, note, or reminder

Rule #2: **Seek feedback** on your practice.

1. Determine how you want to receive feedback: From a stopwatch? A personal critique? A video?
2. Notice what went well and what could go better, including your reactions and feelings about performance.
3. Commit to accepting feedback as data rather than criticism and be willing to make changes.

Rule #3: **Make Adjustments** to refine your practice.

1. What is the smallest measure of feedback you can re-apply to your goals practice? Reassign **time and kind** actions.
2. What can you do in a new way based on feedback?
3. Engage a friend or mentor who will help keep you feeling motivated rather than defeated.

Reflect

What adjustments do you need to make? Assign yourself the Time and Kind of work that will put them into practice.

This week's practice was:
"Follow the Three Rules for Adulting"
ASK YOURSELF DAILY: What went well today?
                     To get more of this I will . . .

WEEK TWO
Just Get Started Daily

Learn
A dream or wish is an imagined hope for your future. To reach an epic goal you will need more than lots of imagination. To make your wish a reality, you need to set goals effectively. Big goals such as landing your dream job or making it to the Olympics are made up of many smaller goals along the way. People who successfully achieve their goals are not necessarily the most talented. Instead they have something else in common. They know how to assign themselves the time and kind of work that moves them toward their goals, they seek regular feedback, and they make the adjustments that lead to improvement.

Grow
Goals can be exhilarating, especially at the beginning. Managing your time horizon for achieving a goal is important. To successfully reach a goal, you might want to think of it as a work in progress. You may need to work with the end in mind, but you'll also need to continue getting started on it daily, day after day. One of your challenges will be continually believing that your goal is achievable when you face inevitable difficulties. You might slip into thoughts about why it might not happen or even be tempted to give up. Be sure to check your mind chatter. What kind of work is needed to reach your goal? What skills do you already have, and which ones will you want to learn? While it may be true that you cannot be absolutely anything you want to be, reaching your dream is probably well within your reach.

Flourish

CHOOSE A GOAL

Can you imagine yourself wildly successful one to five years from now? Your future story, the one that you will be able to tell when your goal has been reached, can be like a giant magnet that pulls you along the goal pathway of your choice.

1. What would you like to accomplish? Dream big. Write several possible goals and as many desirable accomplishments as you can think of.

2. Now choose one of the items on your list to turn into a goal.

3. Write your commitment statement below. Use the prompt to help you. State the goal in positive language—do not use "not."

    I will (Use action words: achieve, create, complete...)

    by (time, date...)

Reflect

Now that you have stated your goal, what is the first step you will take toward it? What feedback measurement will help you know that you are making progress?

This week's practice was: "Just Get Started Daily"
ASK YOURSELF DAILY: What went well today?
                       To get more of this I will . . .

WEEK THREE

Make a Growth Mindset Goal Plan

Learn

The first action step in any goal plan is to be sure that you are using your Growth Mindset. Remember that this means you believe:

- Learning is a process
- Smart is what you become
- Effort improves your talent
- Practice is the key to better
- Failure means you can learn and can try again

You just have not achieved your goal *yet*. When you feel discouraged, remember the power of yet. It leaves you room for another go, and encourages you to adjust your efforts for a new, improved outcome.

Grow

Performance psychologists have studied what makes people most likely to achieve their goals. Something to ask yourself is this: Are you setting this goal for yourself? Intrinsic goals, the ones that come from inside us, are more motivating than extrinsic goals, the ones set for us by other people. You may have noticed this when an instructor or boss gave you an assignment you would not have chosen for yourself. Compare that feeling to when you really want to accomplish a goal! In this week's Flourish activity, you will use a goal plan interview template to state and refine a goal.

Flourish

MAKE A 10-C'S GOAL PLAN

Focus on your answers to these ten questions. Complete this activity either alone or through an interview. You can change the "I" to "You" if you are asking someone else. Record the answers.

1. **Clear Outcome:** What goal do I/you want to achieve?
2. **Choice:** Why am I/are you attracted to this goal?
3. **Challenge:** Why is this goal a stretch for me/you?
4. **Capacity:** What strengths will help me/you reach this goal?
5. **Critical Feedback:** How will I/you receive meaningful feedback?
6. **Connection:** How will completing this goal help me/you with my/your other goals?
7. **Calculable:** What measurement will show that I/you have completed the goal?
8. **Controllable:** How will I/you stay motivated, if I am/you are discouraged?
9. **Course Correction:** Who will be my/your accountability partner and redirect me/you?
10. **Conclusion:** When will I/you commit to being done?

Reflect

Review your goal plan. What is your start date?

Write it here: _____

This week's practice was:
"Make a Growth Mindset Goal Plan"
ASK YOURSELF DAILY: What went well today?
                         To get more of this I will . . .

WEEK FOUR
Reward Small Wins Regularly

Learn
Whether you have been training for something for your whole life or are just getting started, you can set goals that will help you improve your current performance by noticing small successes. These small wins are ingredients for your future big successes. Small wins add up. They increase your positive emotion bank account. Remember from the Positivity section that happier people find it easier to focus on what's going well, they expect more positive outcomes in the future, and they use their hope and optimism to take action and keep moving forward.

Grow
The best performers also practice by gradually refining particular aspects of their individual performances. This discipline is necessary to get to expert levels. If you are on a team, it also matters to spend extensive time practicing mindfully together and getting regular, immediate feedback from top coaches or teachers who help you set personal strategic goals. Specific individual practice leads to the small wins that everyone needs to succeed. You can get started with an activity that you love. It can help to have passion for the activities involved in reaching your goal, but this is not a requirement of succeeding. You might develop love for an activity by learning something new. That's a small win in itself.

Flourish
REWARDING SMALL WINS

Think about the following statements and respond to the questions about your goal behaviors of this week.

1. Success in any endeavor may require the willingness to push yourself beyond your comfort zone.
   - » Where did you willingly push beyond your comfort zone this week, and what was the result?
2. Success in any endeavor may require participating in training activities, potentially with someone more expert than you and skilled in developing particular abilities.
   - » What specific training steps did you take this week toward achieving your goal? What were the results?
3. Success in any endeavor may require incorporating many kinds of feedback to identify strengths and areas for refinement.
   - » What feedback did you receive, and how did you use it to notice and celebrate your small wins?

Reflect
Every step helps to move you ahead toward your goal, sometimes even ones that don't head in the direction you thought you were heading. What is a surprisingly small step that you took this week that turned out to be more valuable than you expected?

This week's practice was:
"Reward Small Wins Regularly"
ASK YOURSELF DAILY: What went well today?
 To get more of this I will . . .

WEEK FIVE

Be Gritty and Accountable

Learn
Until Sir Roger Bannister ran a mile in under four minutes, many people believed that no person could run that fast. People had been running for millions of years, of course, but Bannister did not reach this goal and break this record until 1954. Once people believed they could also run that fast (growth mindset!) Bannister's record lasted only 46 days. When you see great performances, whether they are in sports, arts, or technology, you may not know how many tiny steps and multiple failures preceded the astounding success. The potential to improve your performance exists as long as you believe you can, and you continue to practice. Some performances have just not happened yet.

Grow
Getting started on your goal plan may seem easy at first. You might be motivated by self-improvement, or competition might inspire you to work toward achieving new goals. The first day you'll just get started. But a few days into your plan you might find your motivation is lacking. While you may not be able to recapture the zest and enthusiasm of starting on the very first day, you can plan ahead for lack of motivation by having an accountability partner. This person will not feel sorry for you, will not give you permission to quit, will expect you to show up and succeed, and will not shame you. Your accountability partner is an essential part of your success team.

Flourish

PLAN AHEAD FOR PERSEVERANCE PROBLEMS

Here is your task: Choose and ask someone to be your accountability partner.

1. Explain your goal to this person and share your 10-C's Goal Plan with them.

2. Say that you expect to need help with achieving it, and that you want them on your team.

3. Affirm your commitment and plan. For example, if you don't want to practice, then you will contact your Accountability Partner (A.P).

4. Provide your A.P. a list of several things that can help you get back on track, such as:

   a. Help me savor the future. Remind me of how it will make me feel to achieve my goal of _____.

   b. Set a time after I am to have completed my goal of _____ when we will meet up for a fun activity.

   c. Meet me at the practice time and place and take a photo or video of my performance. Text it to me with a "You did it!" message.

   d. Let me text you if I don't want to practice. Respond, "Say more about that." Ask me to explain why I really do want to practice.

   e. If I miss a scheduled practice, don't criticize or shame me. Ask me to put the next date and time on my calendar.

Reflect

Who else do you want to have on your success team? Remember that they need to believe you want to accomplish your goal. Don't pick someone who will whine with you or criticize you. You want someone to challenge your negative mind chatter and expect you to show up to work toward success. Go, team!

Who did you choose? What are their qualifications for being your A.P.?

_____

_____

This week's practice was: "Be Gritty and Accountable"
ASK YOURSELF DAILY: What went well today?
To get more of this I will . . .

EXTEND YOUR GOALSETTING, GRIT, GROWTH MINDSET
» -Plan for and stick with what's good
» -Unleash the power of YET

THE 10 C'S FOR GOAL SETTING

Each of the ten questions below helps you bust the effort myth by infusing your skills, choices, and self-direction into the goal. Every time you have a goal to achieve, you can use this chart to fine-tune your approach.

Question	Your Answer
1. **Clear Outcome**: What do I want to achieve?	
2. **Choice**: Why am I attracted to this goal?	
3. **Challenge**: Why is this goal a stretch for me?	
4. **Capacity**: What strengths do I have for reaching this goal?	
5. **Critical Feedback**: How will I receive meaningful (data) feedback?	
6. **Connection**: How will completing this goal help me with my other goals?	
7. **Calculable**: What measurement will show that I have completed the goal?	
8. **Controllable**: How will I stay motivated, if I am discouraged?	
9. **Course Correction**: Who will be my accountability partner and redirect me?	
10. **Conclusion**: When will I commit to being done?	

SECTION SEVEN:
ENGAGEMENT AND EXERCISE

KEYS TO ENGAGEMENT AND EXERCISE
» Apply strengths and mindfulness.
» Invest in shared experiences.

Engagement is the experience you have when your strengths meet your challenges. This can happen in nearly any part of your life. People also call this state of mind-body-spirit connection being in "flow". When you are in flow you are full of positive energy and completely involved in an activity. Your intense, focused concentration on the "now" point makes you forget about time, and both performing and learning can take place without your conscious awareness. Activities performed while you use strengths, such as participation in the arts, sports, games, or creative hobbies are natural ways to seek flow and be engaged. It's like zoning in (as opposed to zoning out).

When you perform well and still do not come out a winner, you can be plagued by blame and self-doubt. Mindfulness, another way of being engaged, has many benefits. An important one is that it allows you to recognize your feelings, suspend judgment, and stop attending to your mind chatter, even if only for a short while. Mindful awareness is a tool for helping you regain calm and focus. The simplest meditations involve only something you already do an average of 12 to 20 times every minute—breathe.

Remember that your mind and body are a team, and they give each other feedback through an elegant system of thoughts, emotions, actions, and biochemicals. Keeping that system well fed, rested, and moving supports your well-being and your POS-EDGE.

Engagement and Exercise Practices

WEEK ONE

Practice Mindfulness Meditation

WEEK TWO

Focus on Food, Exercise, and Sleep

WEEK THREE

Move: It's Good Medicine

WEEK FOUR

Get Into Flow

WEEK FIVE

Invest in Experiences

WEEK ONE
Practice Mindfulness Meditation

Learn
Some people think that they cannot learn to meditate and have many excuses for not even getting started. They say things like, "I can't stop thinking about things." "I don't have the time." "I don't have the discipline." "I can't sit still." This is despite the fact that the basic skill of meditating is simple breathing, which you do all day, every day! You already know that you can do that. By training your breath you can use it for more than respiration. People who meditate benefit from many positive effects of their practice.

Grow
Mindfulness meditation transforms your moods, thoughts, emotions, behaviors, and health. It includes three levels. Each time you practice mindfulness, you will begin with the first level, using the breath to guide you to focus. You might be certain that you cannot quiet your noisy mind. Remember that everyone would be unfocused all the time if they did not have a skill to manage that! Breathing techniques and practice will lead you to the second level, where you can eventually be aware of thoughts but not really need to think about them while meditating. You'll be building well-being while on the way to Level 3.

Level 1
Unfocused, concentrating on mind chatter and intrusive thoughts

Level 2
Focused, concentrating on the "now" by noticing and releasing thoughts

Level 3
Open, aware of intuitive clarity, calm, and connection

Flourish

STANDING BODY SCAN MEDITATION

You can meditate in any posture. Try this standing in bare feet. You can also sit or lie down. Close your eyes most, but not all of the way so you can see the floor in front of you. Take a long, slow, deep breath in through your nose, filling your belly first, then your chest, and then your shoulders. Let it out slowly and completely by mouth. Take three long, slow deep belly breath cycles this way. Keep breathing in and out.

- Now **focus on the soles of your feet**, and notice the sensations you feel there.
- Now **focus on your ankles** and the sensations you feel there.
- Now **focus on your knees** and the sensations you feel there.
- Now **focus on your hips** and the sensations you feel there.
- Now **focus on your belly** and the sensations you feel there.
- Now **focus on your shoulders** and the sensations you feel there.
- Now **focus on your neck** and the sensations you feel there.
- Now **focus on your nose** and on the breath going in and out of you.
- Now **focus on your forehead** and the sensations you feel there.

Slowly open your eyes. Shake out your arms overhead, and shake out one leg at a time. Breathe normally.

Reflect
What was this like for you? Describe your experience.

This week's practice was:
"Practice Mindfulness Meditation"
ASK YOURSELF DAILY: What went well today?
                                         To get more of this I will . . .

WEEK TWO

Focus on Food, Exercise, and Sleep

Learn

In the section on Decision Making, you learned that choices can be complicated. For one thing, you need to be kind to your emotional elephant. Your elephant can overpower your rider in three important areas: food, exercise, and sleep. To prevent this, the elephant needs to know what is expected of it, so keeping the pathway to success consistent and marked with cues is essential. Also, you will need to limit choices so that your logical rider stays focused on the plan and doesn't make seemingly acceptable choices that instead let the distractible elephant off the path.

Grow

We often rush with our meals. This can mean consuming things that are not only unhealthy but are also not very enjoyable to eat. You may hardly notice that you ate at all. One way to eat healthier is to put tempting, easy to gobble but less healthy foods out of sight, like in a cupboard instead of on the counter. Better yet, shop for healthier choices you also like, such as fruits and veggies. Cut up veggies ahead of time. Leave them in clear containers in the fridge where they're easy to see and snack from. A high fiber snack, a big glass of water, and a walk will take the edge off hunger.

Go to sleep at a consistent time, too. Work backwards from the time you need to be up, dressed, and ready to leave, and set your bedtime to give you about eight hours of sleep. Set your alarm so that it repeats at that time every day. Turn off your devices an hour before the bedtime you set. Better yet, silence your device and put it in a drawer where you won't see it until morning. When you are consistently well-rested, every part of your mind and body will benefit. Consistent eating and sleeping habits help build more dependable brain resources and well-being.

Flourish
SLOW FOOD MEDITATION

What if you could discover something about your favorite foods that you never noticed before? For this meditation, choose a small spoonful each of three foods you really like. If you need to, cut up the food into bite-sized pieces. It's okay to be messy! Follow these steps:

1. Start by touching the bits of food one at a time, at first with your fingers. Take your time. Explore.

2. Notice something about each food that you have never seen, felt, or smelled before.

3. Now touch one of them to your tongue, but do not put it all the way into your mouth. Just taste.

4. Put the food onto your tongue and close your mouth, but do not chew yet.

5. Now close your eyes, and then chew very slowly, at least 20 times, before swallowing. Do this with every bite.

Reflect
What was this like for you? How long does it take you to eat three spoonfuls of food? What did you notice about your favorite foods? What's good about that? Describe your experience.

This week's practice was:
"Focus on Food, Exercise, and Sleep"
ASK YOURSELF DAILY: What went well today?
 To get more of this I will . . .

WEEK THREE

Move: It's Good Medicine

Learn
In places in the world where humans live the longest and healthiest lives, people share some important lifestyle similarities. One of these is that they have days full of natural movement, including walking, bicycle riding, and hiking. People who live in these places around the world, called Blue Zones, are not just physically healthier. They are also emotionally healthier and have stronger cognitive (thinking) health even as they age into their 90's and beyond. Scientists have found that movement like this is not only good for your physical health and sport performance; it's essential for your well-being.

Grow
You probably know that regular aerobic exercise, the kind that increases your heart rate, is an essential part of your conditioning workout. Researchers have found that cardio exercise before learning, like in the morning before school or work, also helps you have better memory and learning skills, as well as be more focused and effective. Exercising brains send out chemicals telling your body to grow new brain cells and to make the new brain connections you'll need to make good use of those cells. The parts of your brain responsible for focused attention are also made more active by exercise. People who exercise are also less likely to be depressed. All of these are important wins.

ENGAGEMENT AND EXERCISE

Flourish

REFINE YOUR GOALS

For this activity, add natural movement to each day.

   a. If you have a movement tracker, wearable device, or smartphone see how far you are going per day on average.

2. What activities besides walking could increase your natural movement? How many steps would it take for your steps to add up to 10,000 or more a day? (10,000 steps is about 5 miles, but you don't need to do all 10,000 at once.)

3. Make a goal-setting plan to help you increase your daily step total. Choose a reasonable target to begin with, such as 500 or 1000 more steps a day while you build up to 10,000.

Reflect

Remember that people in the Blue Zones include walking, bicycle riding, and hill climbing, spread throughout the daily natural movement in their lives. They also get outside in nature. What are the most likely ways you can continue to add movement to your daily life?

This week's practice was: "Move: It's Good Medicine"
ASK YOURSELF DAILY: What went well today?
                        To get more of this I will . . .

WEEK FOUR
....
Get Into Flow

Learn
Discovering where you have opportunities for flow is one way to build well-being into your everyday life. What is something that comes easily to you? Think of something that you are willing to practice over and over again just to polish your performance. You must want to do this task without being reminded. Flow activities require a performance challenge beyond your average ones, with a measurable goal, and a structure such as a regular time and place to practice what you choose. Also, you'll need the growth mindset belief that you can try the task at hand while taking in feedback and making adjustments.

Grow
The flow state is an opportunity for optimal growth. Instead of critiquing yourself on video or undertaking repetitive exercises, choose challenging activities to engage in for their own sake. When you are in flow, you are able to notice and evaluate your actions while making small changes to improve your performance. While you are running, spinning, or kicking you will be asking yourself, "How well am I doing?" and "What must I do next?" to smoothly make changes. This well-being building experience is so self-absorbing that you will not notice time going by. Only afterwards will you know that you were in flow.

Flourish
RIG YOUR PRACTICE

One way to get into flow more often is to rig your practice to make it a little more challenging. Start with a clear goal that's important to you. Add structure with rules to control time and difficulty. Change things like the scenery, location, route, sequence, or speed when you practice. Be sure that you will get immediate feedback from a person or device so that you can automatically respond and change on the way to your goal. The first few times you try this, make your time open-ended so that you can both get into flow and stay there.

Reflect
- What goal did you choose to make more challenging?
- How did you change the structure and rules for practicing?
- What kind of feedback did you notice? Did you lose track of time?
- How did you feel right after practicing, or even a day or two later?
- How can you tweak your activities to get more flow?

This week's practice was: "Get Into Flow"
ASK YOURSELF DAILY: **What went well today?**
To get more of this I will . . .

WEEK FIVE

Invest in Experiences

Learn
Sometimes life events may lead you to struggle more than you would expect. You may become depleted and find yourself tempted by a small quick pleasure now, even though waiting and considering your future health is a much better long-term strategy. You have learned many ways to stay gritty and choose the long view. There is a saying about mindfulness practices: "Every day is different." It is also good to remember this when you have worked hard toward your goals of meditating, eating, sleeping, and exercising well.

Grow
At the beginning of your workbook you learned how to be grateful for what is going well, and to savor that. Instead of catastrophizing, you learned to focus on the most likely future and do things within your power to get you there. When you needed to be yourself at your best, you used your star strengths and their sidekicks. Instead of letting your emotional elephant stray from the right path and mindlessly choose short term pleasure, you have invested in meaningful times with friends and family. You've reached out to your accountability partner when you needed to get back on track with goals.

Flourish
BE AWED BY EXPERIENCING BEAUTY AND EXCELLENCE

Two other ways you can improve your well-being are by going into nature, and by watching excellent human performances. People who experience awe in their lives in this way can increase their feelings of gratitude and meaningfulness. What things in your life inspire you to have feelings of awe?

1. Find a place that you find awe-inspiring. It can be in the natural world, or be a human creation or performance.

2. Take a long slow deep breath to get into a mindful state, and let yourself be inspired.

3. Afterwards write about what you experienced.

Reflect
When you want to be deeply engaged in an experience, what are the things you choose? List a variety of them from concerts, movies, sports, and outdoor adventures, to books, travel, and family celebrations.

This week's practice was: "Invest in Experiences"
ASK YOURSELF DAILY: What went well today?
To get more of this I will . . .

EXTEND YOUR ENGAGEMENT AND EXERCISE
» Apply strengths and mindfulness
» Invest in shared experiences

THE MINDFUL PAUSE

Here is a practice that you can try right after an energetic, flow-filled workout to pause and then bring yourself back to a focused, ready state for engagement.

There are three steps:

1. **Relax:** Down-regulate. Create calm and focus in your body and brain.

    Sit still. Close your eyes. Breathe slowly and deeply—in through the nose/out through the mouth. Take your time. Three minutes is about right.

2. **Release:** Notice and then let go of thoughts that pop into your head.

    You don't have to push them away. Let them be like clouds that are just blowing through your mind to reveal a clear sky.

3. **Re-engage:** Up-regulate with "eight to concentrate".

    When you are ready, stand up slowly. Inhale while slowly sweeping your arms overhead and exhale them down again. Use "eight to concentrate": Do this 8x to gently up-regulate and energize your brain for learning, working, and connecting.

When/Where/How I did this: _____

_____

I noticed that: _____

_____

My next practice session will be _____

_____

Appendix

My POS-EDGE Profile: Unleashing My Epic Self

Positivity (P)
- » Notice what's good.
- » Collect more positive than negative.

Optimism and resilience (O)
- » Expect what's good.
- » Reframe what isn't.

Strengths (S)
- » Get more of what's good about you.
- » Develop new strengths.

Emotional intelligence (E)
- » Develop solid relationships.
- » Be grateful, forgiving, and kind.

Decision making and change (D)
- » Desire what's good.
- » Manage obstacles to success.

Goal setting, grit, and growth mindset (G)
- » Plan for and stick with what's good.
- » Unleash the power of YET.

Engagement and exercise (E)
- » Apply strengths and mindfulness.
- » Invest in shared experiences.

Review and Reflect

It's time to reflect on the powerful learning journey you've recorded in your mind, your body, and in this workbook. Going back through your writing, activities, and reflections, what are the times when you were at your best? Choose the highlights from your UYES workbook and write them. Read the statements and write how you achieved each one:

(P) My positivity investments have appreciated. I am happier and more grateful.

(O) I have imagined my best future self. I expect the good and reframe negative mind chatter.

(S) I can harness my strengths to unleash my epic self. I have worked to develop what's best about me.

(E) My high quality relationships matter. I have strengthened my people connections.

(D) I go with what works to build habits. I rig my decisions for greatness.

(G) I have invested in self-directed hard work over time. My mindset reminds me that I can improve.

(E) I can breathe to focus on now. I choose healthy sleeping, eating, and exercise to build my well-being.

Character Strengths

- creativity
- curiosity
- judgment
- love of learning
- perspective
- bravery
- perseverance
- honesty
- zest
- love
- kindness
- social intelligence
- teamwork
- fairness
- leadership
- forgiveness
- humility
- prudence
- self-regulation
- appreciation of beauty and excellence
- gratitude
- hope
- humor
- spirituality

For more information and to take the VIA Character Strengths Survey see www.viacharacter.org

VIA Youth Survey ©Copyright 2004-2022, VIA Institute on Character. All Rights Reserved. Used with permission.

Inspiration and Gratitude

The goal of this workbook is for you, your communities and the world you live in to benefit from the many practical and preventative benefits of well-being. I could not have written it for you without studying the work of many forward-thinking professional researchers and practitioners. Some of them have retired, or passed from this world. While I recognize that this is not an exhaustive list, I have been especially inspired by the work of the people below:

Fred Bryant, PhD
Savoring

Mihaly Csikszentmihalyi, PhD
Flow

Edward Deci, PhD
Self-determination Theory

Ed Diener, PhD
Subjective Well-being

Charles Duhigg
Habits

Angela Duckworth, PhD
Grit

Carol Dweck, PhD
Mindset

Robert A. Emmons, PhD
Gratitude

Barbara Fredrickson, PhD
Positivity

Jane Gillham, PhD
Resilience

Adam Grant, PhD
Positive Organizations

Jonathan Haidt, PhD
Social Intuition

Scott Barry Kaufman, PhD
Creativity and Intelligence

Peggy Kern, PhD
PERMA Profiler

Shane Lopez, PhD
Hope

Sonja Lyubomirsky, PhD
Happiness

Kristin Neff, PhD
Mindful and Compassionate Living

Christopher Peterson, PhD
Character Strengths

Tayyab Rashid, PhD
Strengths and Mental Health

Timothy Pychyl, PhD
Procrastination

John Ratey, MD
Exercise

Tom Rath, MAPP
Wellbeing

Karen Reivich, PhD
Optimism and Resilience

Martin Seligman, PhD
PERMA Well-being Model

Emma Seppala, PhD
Mindfulness

Lea Waters, PhD
Strengths and Positive Functioning

Jon Kabat-Zinn
Mindfulness Based Stress Reduction

Zen Master Thich Nhat Hanh
Mindfulness & Peace

About the Author

 Sherri Fisher has dedicated decades to challenging the Effort Myth, both in schools and private practice. She believes that no one should have to suffer to be able to learn. Parents who work with Sherri in their youth return with their own children. Her client relationships don't just span grades; they span generations.

As a learning specialist and executive coach for students and their parents, Sherri has pioneered research-based tools that build skilled resilience, motivation, and self-direction. As a schools consultant she has guided educators and administrators to nurture the flexibility, strengths, and relationships that help improve academic and life outcomes.

Sherri is the Director of Learn & Flourish, an education coaching and consulting firm with clients on five continents. She earned her Master's degree in Applied Positive Psychology from the University of Pennsylvania where she studied with the founders of the field. Sherri lives in New England where she raised her children, her gardens, and her pack of friendly dogs.

For more information visit http://learnandflourish.com

www.ingramcontent.com/pod-product-compliance
Lightning Source LLC
Chambersburg PA
CBHW071902070526
44583CB00016B/1810